KEY QUESTIONS
in AMERICAN HISTORY

DID THE
ABOLITION
MOVEMENT
ABOLISH SLAVERY?

JOAN STOLTMAN

PowerKiDS
press

New York

Published in 2019 by The Rosen Publishing Group, Inc.
29 East 21st Street, New York, NY 10010

First Edition

Editor: Elizabeth Krajnik
Book Design: Tanya Dellaccio

Photo Credits: Cover, back cover, pp. 1, 3-32 (background) Tatiana Kasyanova/Shutterstock.com; cover, back cover, pp. 5, 6, 9, 11, 13, 15, 17, 18, 21, 25, 29 (newspaper clipping) STILLFX/Shutterstock.com; cover (Harriet Beecher Stowe) Historical/Corbis Historical/Getty Images; cover (Frederick Douglass) Library of Congress/Getty Images; cover (Emancipation Proclamation meeting) Bettmann/Getty Images; p. 5 (Underground Railroad map) Interim Archives/Archive Photos/Getty Images; p. 5 (Andrew Jackson) Everett - Art/Shutterstock.com; p. 7 (Thomas Clarkson) Georgios Kollidas/Shutterstock.com; p. 7 (slave ship poster) https://commons.wikimedia.org/wiki/File:Slaveshipposter.jpg; p. 9 (safe house) MPI/Archive Photos/Getty Images; p. 9 (Methodist Camp) Lawrence Thornton/Archive Photos/Getty Images; p. 11 Fotosearch/Archive Photos/Getty Images; p. 13 (Uncle Tom's Cabin cover) https://commons.wikimedia.org/wiki/File:UncleTomsCabinCover.jpg; p. 13 (slave poster), 19 (slave poster), 21 (John Brown's fort) Courtesy of the Library of Congress; p. 14 MPI/Archive Photos/Getty Images; p. 15 (statue) MCT/Tribune News Service/Getty Images; pp. 15 (Sojourner Truth), 17, 23, 27 (Emancipation Proclamation meeting), 29 Everett Historical/Shutterstock.com; p. 19 (illustration) Photo 12/Universal Images Group/Getty Images; p. 21 (illustration) Hulton Archive/Getty Images; p. 25 (Fort Wagner) https://upload.wikimedia.org/wikipedia/commons/8/86/The_Storming_of_Ft_Wagner-lithograph_by_Kurz_and_Allison_1890.jpg; p. 25 (Fort Sumter) Fine Art/Corbis Historical/Getty Images; p. 27 (House of Representatives Celebrating) MPI/Getty Images.

Library of Congress Cataloging-in-Publication Data

Names: Stoltman, Joan, author.
Title: Did the abolition movement abolish slavery? / Joan Stoltman.
Description: New York : PowerKids Press, 2019. | Series: Key questions in American history | Includes index.
Identifiers: LCCN 2017050170| ISBN 9781508167501 (library bound) | ISBN 9781508167525 (pbk.) | ISBN 9781508167532 (6 pack)
Subjects: LCSH: Antislavery movements–United States–History–Juvenile literature. | Slavery–United States–History–Juvenile literature. | Fugitive slaves–United States–History–Juvenile literature. | Abolitionists–United States–History–Juvenile literature.
Classification: LCC E449 .S89585 2019 | DDC 326/.80973–dc23
LC record available at https://lccn.loc.gov/2017050170

Manufactured in the United States of America

CPSIA Compliance Information: Batch #CS18PK: For Further Information contact Rosen Publishing, New York, New York at 1-800-237-9932

CONTENTS

WHAT IS ABOLITION?

Throughout history, slavery has existed in many civilizations. In many of these civilizations, there were also people working against it. In U.S. history, the people who worked together to abolish, or put an end to, slavery are called abolitionists.

Because we weren't alive when slavery existed in the United States, we can only find out what happened by reading accounts from people who were there. However, different people often interpret events in different ways. For example, ex-slave Frederick Douglass spoke of the horrors of slavery. But Southern plantation owners who owned slaves said they kindly provided food and shelter to slaves. We have to study every side of the story to reveal the truth. What is the truth about the U.S. abolitionist movement? Did it truly abolish slavery?

FUGITIVE SLAVES USED UNDERGROUND RAILROAD ROUTES IN 14 NORTHERN STATES TO GET TO CANADA, WHERE SLAVE HUNTERS WOULDN'T BE ABLE TO CAPTURE THEM.

ROUTES OF THE
UNDERGROUND
RAILROAD
1830 - 1865
led from "The Underground Railroad from

The Underground Railroad was the code name for a system slaves used to escape slavery. The first railroads had just been built in the United States, so railroad terms were used to disguise the true nature of these routes. The Underground Railroad wasn't formally organized and didn't officially start on a certain date. Rather, it was a system of people who all had a common goal: to help slaves escape the South.

HISTORIC MOMENTS

Andrew Jackson is one of eight presidents who owned slaves while in office. His plantation had more than 100 slaves.

ANDREW JACKSON

5

ABOLITIONISTS IN ENGLAND

England was one of the main countries involved in building the Atlantic slave trade. By 1810, the slave trade had taken nearly 3 million Africans from their homes and torn many families apart. However, new religious and economic influences began turning many people in England against slavery. In 1807, a law banned the slave trade throughout the British Empire. In 1828, the Abolition of the Slave Trade Act freed almost all slaves in the British Empire.

After this, English abolitionists decided to fight to end slavery worldwide. English lawyer Sir William Blackstone said that "it is repugnant [disgusting] to reason, and the principles of natural law, that such a state [of slavery] should subsist [exist] anywhere." England's laws inspired many Americans to become abolitionists.

the 2...1-02 ...son.

HISTORIC MOMENTS

Some slave traders claimed the Bible says slavery is allowed if slaves are cared for. They said this to make slavery seem like a good thing. However, slaves weren't treated well at all.

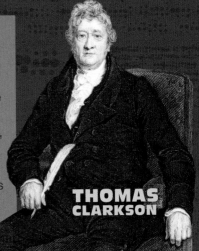

PROVING SLAVERY IS CRUEL

Thomas Clarkson, an English abolitionist, decided to gather evidence to prove slavery was cruel and to get people to support the abolitionist movement. He interviewed over 20,000 people and collected equipment from slave ships, including handcuffs, leg **shackles**, a device used to crush fingers, **branding irons**, and more. Clarkson's research and lectures turned abolition into a major political movement. He helped set up 1,200 branches of an abolition group.

THOMAS CLARKSON

AT LECTURES, CLARKSON OFTEN USED THIS DRAWING TO SHOW HOW SLAVES WERE STORED LIKE CARGO IN SLAVE SHIPS. HE WOULD ALSO OFTEN SHOW THE SLAVE SHIP EQUIPMENT HE'D COLLECTED. PEOPLE WERE HORRIFIED—AND MANY BECAME ABOLITIONISTS AS A RESULT.

PLAN OF LOWER DECK WITH THE STOWAGE OF 292 SLAVES
130 OF THESE BEING STOWED UNDER THE SHELVES AS SHEWN IN FIGURE D & FIGURE 5.

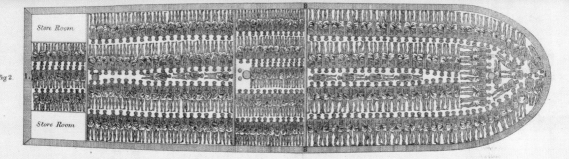

Fig 2.

Store Room

Store Room

PLAN SHEWING THE STOWAGE OF 130 ADDITIONAL SLAVES ROUND THE WINGS OR SIDES OF THE LOWER DECK BY MEANS OF PLATFORMS OR SHELVES (IN THE MANNER OF GALLERIES IN A CHURCH) THE SLAVES STOWED ON THE SHELVES AND BELOW THEM HAVE ONLY A HEIGHT OF 2 FEET 7 INCHES BETWEEN THE BEAMS: AND FAR LESS UNDER THE BEAMS. See Fig 1.

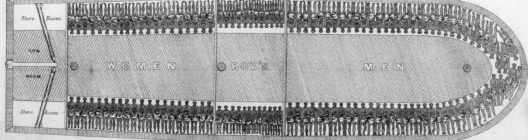

Fig 3.

Store Room

GUN ROOM

Store Room

WOMEN   BOY'S   MEN

7

RELIGION TURNS
TO ACTION

Slavery existed in North America in colonial times and, with it, people who were against the practice. Members of a religious group called the Mennonites wrote against slavery in 1688, stating, "We should do to all men like as we will be done ourselves; making no difference of what generation, descent, or colour they are." But abolition wasn't a widespread public cause in the United States until the Second Great Awakening of the 1800s. This was a religious movement that encouraged a strong sense of right and wrong and encouraged people to actively and publicly fight for what they believed in.

Many people were **galvanized** when abolitionists claimed their cause was morally right and should be supported by all Christians. Slave owners, they explained, didn't work for what they earned and slaves were humans created by God.

THE SECOND GREAT AWAKENING BEGAN IN NEW ENGLAND IN THE 1790s. THIS IMAGE SHOWS THE GREAT METHODIST CAMP MEETING, WHICH RAN FROM AUGUST 20 TO AUGUST 26, 1865, IN SING SING, NEW YORK.

THE QUAKERS

The Quakers, members of a religious group founded in England in the mid-1600s, are mentioned often in the history of England and the United States' abolitionist movements. In 1688, a group of four male Quakers from Germantown, Pennsylvania, wrote and signed a petition, or formal written request made to an official group, protesting slavery. In 1774, the Quakers officially banned their members from owning slaves or participating in the slave trade. By the 1840s, about 250,000 Americans belonged to over 2,000 abolitionist societies—and most of those people were Quakers.

the 2... ...on.

HISTORIC MOMENTS

In 1832, Thomas Roderick Dew, an academic and a supporter of slavery from Virginia, published *Review of the Debate in the Virginia Legislature of 1831 and 1832*. This book examined slavery in the United States and often supported it. However, some of what Dew said in his book went against what he had previously said about slavery.

SPREADING THE WORD

Abolitionists came from all backgrounds—black, white, free, slave, northern, and even southern. This made for a wide variety of goals. Some wanted gradual abolition, while others wanted immediate abolition. Some suggested that slave owners be paid for their lost "property" after abolition; others thought payment was owed to the slaves. Some even demanded full **racial equality**, though that was an extreme position to most abolitionists.

Regardless of what type of abolition they fought for, many felt the focus of the movement should be to convert the masses. They did this by writing pamphlets, or short printed publications, books, **autobiographies**, plays, and essays. Others felt it was more important to change the laws. Still others focused on helping slaves escape. A few abolitionists felt the only solution was violence.

THE LARGEST ABOLITIONIST GROUP, THE AMERICAN ANTI-SLAVERY SOCIETY, OR AASS, MAILED 385,000 PAMPHLETS IN 1835. PEOPLE AGAINST ABOLITION ATTACKED POST OFFICES TO BURN THE PAMPHLETS AND ANY NEWSPAPERS OR MAIL COMING FROM THE NORTH.

HISTORIC MOMENTS

An 1829 essay by David Walker, a free black man, argued against colonization. He wrote to his fellow blacks: "America is more our country than it is the whites'—we have enriched [improved] it with our blood and tears."

COLONIZATION

Some whites feared that free blacks wanted social and political equality. Within the abolitionist movement, there was a belief that **prejudices** were too strong to ever allow equality. Some people believed that the answer was **colonization**, or sending all blacks to Africa. The American Colonization Society bought land in west Africa and offered it to former slaves. By 1860, 15,000 had moved, but this was only a small portion of the 4 million former slaves.

THE PRINTED WORD

Many abolitionist newspapers were established during the movement. William Lloyd Garrison published the *Liberator*, a weekly abolitionist newspaper, for 35 years. In 1835, he was dragged through the streets by a mob of white people who said he was pushing racial **integration** or, even worse, equality. Another hostile mob murdered abolitionist newspaper editor Elijah P. Lovejoy in 1837. Abolitionists gained many new supporters because Lovejoy's murder shocked people.

Harriet Beecher Stowe's 1852 fiction book *Uncle Tom's Cabin* spread the abolitionist message far and wide, selling more copies that century than any other book except the Bible. William Still, a free black man often called the father of the Underground Railroad, wrote *The Underground Railroad Records*. The book is a collection of the stories of 649 slaves he helped escape via the Underground Railroad.

HISTORIC MOMENTS

In 1833, there were four abolitionist groups in the United States. The following year, there were 47. By 1838, there were about 1,300 abolitionist groups.

STUDENTS READ *UNCLE TOM'S CABIN* IN SCHOOLS ACROSS AMERICA TODAY. TEACHERS USE THE BOOK TO SHOW HOW THE WRITTEN WORD CAN AFFECT THE PUBLIC'S OPINION OF A CERTAIN TOPIC.

UNCLE TOM'S CABIN;

OR,

LIFE AMONG THE LOWLY.

BY

HARRIET BEECHER STOWE.

VOL. I.

ONE HUNDRED AND FIFTH THOUSAND.

BOSTON:
JOHN P. JEWETT & COMPANY
CLEVELAND, OHIO:
JEWETT, PROCTOR & WORTHINGTON.
1852.

OUR COUNTRYMEN IN CHAINS.

AM I NOT A MAN AND A BROTHER?

AN ABOLITIONIST POEM

"What, ho!—our countrymen in chains!—
The whip on WOMAN'S shrinking flesh!
Our soil yet reddening with the stains,
Caught from her scourging [whipping], warm and fresh!
What! mothers from their children riven [separated]!—
What! God's own image bought and sold!—
AMERICANS to market driven,
And bartered [exchanged] as the brute [beast] for gold!"
—part of John Greenleaf Whittier's poem "Our Countrymen in Chains"

FAMOUS
FORMER SLAVES

Frederick Douglass, a former slave, is one of the most famous African American lecturers and abolitionists in U.S. history. While enslaved, Douglass was taught to read and write in secret by his owner's wife. He escaped and later published a famous autobiography, *Narrative of the Life of Frederick Douglass*. One of the reasons he published his story was to inspire people to become abolitionists.

Henry Bibb, another escaped slave, also published an autobiography, *Narrative of the Life and Adventures of Henry Bibb*. It was less well known than Douglass's but no less powerful. After trying for three years to save his wife and child from slavery, Bibb was forced to give up. He later settled in Canada. There, he founded Canada's first black newspaper, *Voice of the Fugitive*.

HENRY BIBB

Sojourner Truth: In Her Own Words

By the time she was 13 years old, Sojourner Truth had been sold three times. By the time she was 29 years old, she had managed to escape to the North. Bookstores refused to sell her 1850 autobiography, *Narrative of Sojourner Truth: A Northern Slave*, so she spent years traveling and selling it herself. As she traveled, she lectured on abolition and women's rights. After the Civil War, she spoke about the continued violence against former slaves.

SOJOURNER TRUTH

WHITE MEMBERS OF THE AASS CRITICIZED FREDERICK DOUGLASS FOR INCLUDING TALES OF RACISM IN THE NORTH IN HIS LECTURES. THEY WANTED THOSE LEFT OUT.

STATUE OF FREDERICK DOUGLASS

HISTORIC MOMENTS

Abolitionists built Pennsylvania Hall in 1838 because they weren't allowed to host events in any other building in Philadelphia. Four days after it was built, a mob of anti-abolitionists burned the building down.

POWERFUL SPEAKERS

Douglass and Truth weren't the only former slaves to become famous public speakers. Henry Highland Garnet was another prominent African American of the time and an AASS leader. One of the few African Americans to support colonization, Garnet became widely known for an 1843 speech at the National Negro Convention in which he called upon slaves to murder their owners. Many abolitionists withdrew their support for him after this.

Other women also proved powerful speakers. The Grimké sisters were born into a wealthy, slave-owning family in South Carolina, and they witnessed the abuse of their family's slaves many times. Angelina Grimké was the first American woman ever to address a legislative body when she spoke out against slavery in 1838 in Massachusetts. The Grimkés and other women also fought for women's right to vote.

HISTORIC MOMENTS

The U.S. Supreme Court ruled that slaves had no rights in the 1857 Dred Scott case. Dred Scott was born into slavery and tried to buy his and his wife's freedom from his former master's wife. She refused and Scott started legal proceedings to gain his freedom.

Frederick Douglass: In His Own Words

In an 1852 speech about celebrations on Independence Day, Douglass spoke harshly of white Americans, many of whom spent the day celebrating liberty and pride in their nation. Slaves, on the other hand, felt a cruel lack of justice that day more than all others, Douglass said. He called white Americans' pride in themselves and their nation "a thin veil to cover up crimes which would disgrace [shame] a nation of savages."

LAWS THAT
NEEDED TO CHANGE

As abolitionism rose, slave owners in the South pushed for laws to protect their interests. One of the worst was the Fugitive Slave Act of 1850. This law made it easier for people to catch escaped slaves and return them to slavery. If an escaped slave was caught, they weren't given a trial by jury. When fugitive slave Anthony Burns was captured under the law, abolitionists called President Franklin Pierce the "chief slave-catcher of the United States" and threatened him with **assassination**.

People who helped a slave could be jailed, so many abolitionists went to jail. The abolitionists' cause was strengthened by the increasingly harsh laws. This frightened many in the South, who responded by pushing for more laws. Each side grew more upset with the other. These feelings would soon be one of the causes of the Civil War.

HISTORIC MOMENTS

Many states had laws in place to prevent slaves from learning how to read or write. A Virginia law said that if a slave didn't leave the state within a year of being freed, they could be returned to slavery.

THE GAG RULE

Petitions allow for citizens' concerns to be heard in Congress. Abolitionists often petitioned to make sure their cause was heard and remembered. Southern congressmen—and northern congressmen who didn't want to pick a side—passed the Gag Rule of 1836 to make antislavery petitions illegal in Congress. The AASS responded by sending about 682,000 petitions to Congress in 1837. The rule lasted until 1844, when northern congressmen fearing the South's increased power voted against the rule.

IN 1781, LUKE COLLINGWOOD, THE CAPTAIN OF THE SLAVE SHIP *ZONG*, THREW 133 SICK AFRICANS OVERBOARD AND FILED A REPORT TO GET BACK THE VALUE OF THE MURDERED SLAVES. TO ABOLITIONISTS' DISGUST, THE COURT CASE FOCUSED ON THE MONEY, NOT THE MURDERS.

19

THE ECONOMICS OF SLAVERY

It seems obvious today that slavery is evil, so why did the South work so hard to protect it? Cotton and tobacco only grow in certain climates and they require a lot of physical labor to produce. The South had the perfect climate for these crops and slave labor to harvest them. Some southerners thought slavery was a good thing because it supplied the country with products made using these crops.

One North Carolina man of the time said, "the southern people might as well attempt to build a railroad to the moon as to cultivate [grow crops in] their swamp lands without slaves." Because slaves weren't paid, slavery allowed slave owners to save money while making money. Some southerners even said slavery was a good thing because it made sure black people were taken care of.

MANY PEOPLE BOUGHT PRODUCTS SLAVERY HELPED TO PRODUCE. BUYING THESE PRODUCTS FED MONEY BACK INTO SYSTEMS OF SLAVERY, ALLOWING IT TO CONTINUE AND GIVING IT ECONOMIC POWER.

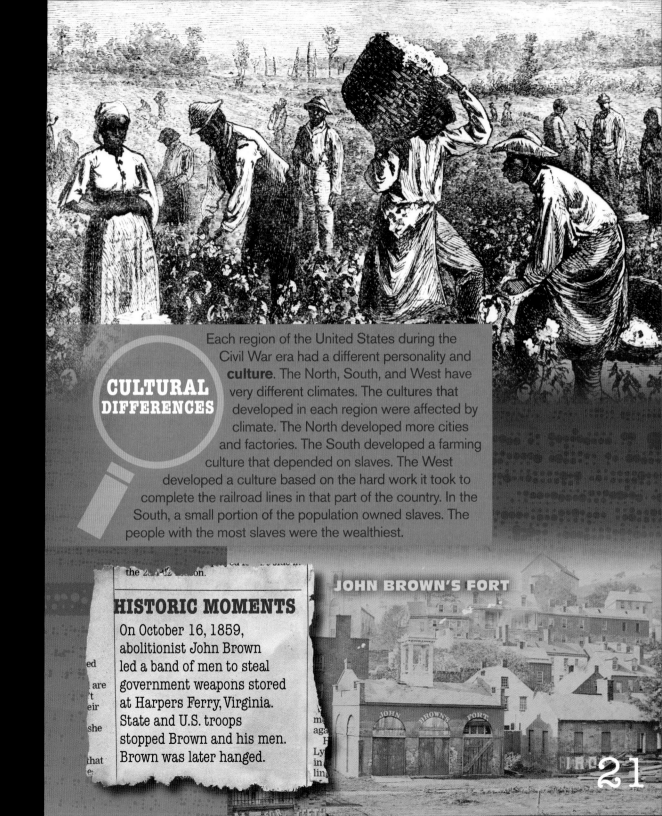

CULTURAL DIFFERENCES

Each region of the United States during the Civil War era had a different personality and **culture**. The North, South, and West have very different climates. The cultures that developed in each region were affected by climate. The North developed more cities and factories. The South developed a farming culture that depended on slaves. The West developed a culture based on the hard work it took to complete the railroad lines in that part of the country. In the South, a small portion of the population owned slaves. The people with the most slaves were the wealthiest.

JOHN BROWN'S FORT

HISTORIC MOMENTS

On October 16, 1859, abolitionist John Brown led a band of men to steal government weapons stored at Harpers Ferry, Virginia. State and U.S. troops stopped Brown and his men. Brown was later hanged.

SECESSION

As the United States continued to expand west, conflict broke out. The Missouri Compromise of 1820 made Missouri a slave state but banned slavery in other western territories north of a certain line. In 1854, the Kansas-Nebraska Act declared that residents of new states would decide the question of slavery themselves. Both sides sent people to the territories, and bloody fights broke out. Since the Missouri Compromise was no longer in effect, abolitionists started ignoring the Fugitive Slave Act, too.

The presidential election of 1860 was a divisive event in U.S. history. Abraham Lincoln won the election, but most of the South voted for John C. Breckinridge. As a result of Lincoln winning the election, 11 southern states eventually seceded, or separated, from the Union and formed their own country, the Confederate States of America. They had their own constitution, capital, printed money, and president—Jefferson Davis.

The Right to Secede

Leaders of the Confederate states believed they had freely joined the United States and therefore could freely leave it. Famous abolitionist lawyer Lysander Spooner agreed. He argued that the Constitution allowed for secession and that the South was only acting as the colonies had in their fight for independence from Britain. He also disagreed with the North declaring war over secession and not over slavery, the real evil.

ANOTHER MAJOR ARGUMENT LEADING UP TO SECESSION WAS HOW MUCH POWER THE FEDERAL GOVERNMENT SHOULD HAVE. MANY IN THE SOUTH FELT STATES SHOULD DECIDE MOST THINGS FOR THEMSELVES AND THAT THE FEDERAL GOVERNMENT SHOULD BE SMALL. MANY IN THE NORTH DISAGREED.

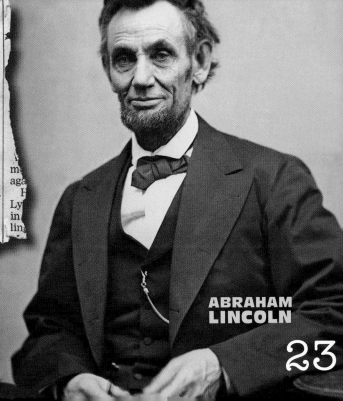

the 2_1-02 season.

HISTORIC MOMENTS

In the 1830s, a Quaker named Benjamin Lundy said he discovered evidence that the South was working to bring slavery to Texas. Even nonabolitionist northerners found this alarming because it meant the slaveowners could soon control more land than the North.

ABRAHAM LINCOLN

A COUNTRY AT WAR

President Lincoln said the South had no right to secede. He said those states were in open rebellion, or resistance against authority. In the South, the American Civil War was called the War of Northern **Aggression** or the War of Southern Independence.

The first outbreak of fighting happened on April 12, 1861, at Fort Sumter in Charleston, South Carolina. At this point, only seven states had seceded—South Carolina, Mississippi, Florida, Alabama, Georgia, Louisiana, and Texas. Just weeks after the 34-hour fight at Fort Sumter, four more states—Virginia, Arkansas, Tennessee, and North Carolina—seceded from the Union.

For four years, the Union and the Confederacy fought. In total, more than 500,000 people died.

the 2...-12 ...on.

HISTORIC MOMENTS

Many Union soldiers wouldn't fight alongside black people. Lincoln was even concerned some border states would secede if black people were allowed to fight. But the North needed men. In 1863, the Union finally allowed black soldiers and seamen.

BLACK MEN SERVED IN SEPARATE GROUPS LED BY WHITE OFFICERS. ONE OF THE MOST FAMOUS WAS THE 54TH MASSACHUSETTS **INFANTRY** REGIMENT. IN ALL, 180,000 BLACK MEN SERVED IN THE UNION ARMY AND 10,000 IN THE UNION NAVY.

FORT WAGNER

A SONG FOR BATTLE

The words to the hymn "Amazing Grace" were written about one man's journey from slave trader to preacher and abolitionist. It became very popular during the Second Great Awakening and also during and after the Civil War. John Newton, the writer, said, "It will always be a subject of humiliating [embarrassing] reflection [memory] to me, that I was once an active instrument in a business at which my heart now shudders."

FORT SUMTER

EMANCIPATION

As the war continued, President Lincoln decided abolition would help the North's cause. It would help frame the war as a battle for freedom and draw former slaves to the Union army. Lincoln's final draft of the Emancipation Proclamation, issued on January 1, 1863, declared slaves in rebel states emancipated, or free.

But because the Confederate states had left the Union, Lincoln's declaration had no power there. The proclamation also didn't free slaves in the border states—Delaware, Maryland, Kentucky, and Missouri—or areas under Union control. Lincoln knew that if he declared emancipation in the border states, they might secede, giving the South more land and more soldiers. Only around 20,000 to 50,000 of over 4 million slaves were freed.

ALTHOUGHT THE EMANCIPATION PROCLAMATION WAS A STEP IN THE DIRECTION OF FREEDOM, SLAVERY WASN'T OFFICIALLY ABOLISHED UNTIL THE RATIFICATION OF THE 13TH AMENDMENT TO THE U.S. CONSTITUTION.

THE 13TH AMENDMENT

The people who remained slaves had to wait until the 13th Amendment for freedom. The 13th Amendment was a change to the Constitution that declared slavery illegal everywhere in the United States. Congress passed the 13th Amendment on January 31, 1865, and it was ratified, or legally approved, by the required amount of states—two-thirds—on December 6, 1865. By this time, the Civil War was over.

27

DID IT WORK?

William Lloyd Garrison declared the abolition movement a success after the 13th Amendment was ratified. However, even though millions of former slaves were free, they weren't considered U.S. citizens until the ratification of the 14th Amendment in 1868. Many abolitionists disagreed that the movement was a success at this time. The AASS continued working through 1870, when the 15th Amendment was ratified, giving black men the right to vote.

For many years after the passage of these three amendments—commonly called the Reconstruction Amendments—some people in the United States worked very hard to prevent African Americans from having the basic rights white people have. Some abolitionists fought for a free and equal society. Even today, that doesn't truly exist.

THIS IMAGE DEPICTS FREED SLAVES MIGRATING TO THE NORTH AFTER THE EMANCIPATION PROCLAMATION WENT INTO EFFECT. AFRICAN AMERICANS CONTINUED MIGRATING NORTH INTO THE MID-20TH CENTURY.

TIMELINE

1775

Pennsylvanians start the first abolition group in the new United States of America.

1833

The American Anti-Slavery Society is formed.

1838

Frederick Douglass escapes slavery.

1838

Narrative of the Life of Frederick Douglass is published seven years after his escape from slavery.

1850

The Fugitive Slave Act requires escaped slaves be returned—dead or alive—to their owners.

MAY 30, 1854

The Kansas–Nebraska Act undoes the Missouri Compromise, allowing territories to choose whether to allow slavery.

MARCH 6, 1857

The U.S. Supreme Court issues the *Dred Scott v. Sanford* decision.

JANUARY 1, 1863

President Abraham Lincoln issues the final draft of the Emancipation Proclamation.

JANUARY 31, 1865

The 13th Amendment is ratified by the required number of states.

GLOSSARY

aggression: Hostile action against someone or something.

assassination: The killing of someone, usually for political reasons.

autobiography: A book that tells the story of a person's life and is written by the person it's about.

branding iron: A tool used to burn a symbol into flesh.

colonization: The movement to establish a colony in Africa for American slaves.

culture: The beliefs and ways of life of a certain group of people.

galvanize: To cause people to become so excited or concerned about an issue, idea, etc., that they want to do something about it.

infantry: A branch of an army composed of soldiers trained to fight on foot.

integration: The act or process of integrating, or making a person or group part of a larger group.

petition: A formal written request.

prejudice: An unfair feeling of dislike for a person or group because of race, sex, or religious or personal beliefs.

racial equality: The concept that all humans regardless of race have the same rights and social status.

racism: The belief that one group or race of people is better than another group or race.

shackle: One of two rings or bands that are placed around a person's wrists or ankles and connected by a chain.

INDEX

WEBSITES

Due to the changing nature of Internet links, PowerKids Press has developed an online
list of websites related to the subject of this book. This site is updated regularly. Please
use this link to access the list: www.powerkidslinks.com/kqah/abolish